Glow

Written by
Noelia González

Illustrated by
Sara Boccaccini Meadows

MAGIC CAT PUBLISHING

Right above our heads, there's an immense window to the cosmos. The night sky allows us to catch a glimpse of what lies beyond the edge of our planet. We don't need much — just our eyes and a handful of curiosity. But do we look up often enough?

From our own back door we can see glowing stars, the awe-inspiring Moon and hypnotic constellations. We might catch elusive shooting stars and even see machines that have been placed in space by humans. We can observe some of our neighbouring worlds in the Solar System, and chunks of the galaxy we live in.

Bright or dim, these celestial objects are cosmic heroes. They exist in inhospitable conditions: withstanding unthinkable cold, heat and radiation, swirling gases and powerful forces. They've been around for many millions of years. They hold clues to our origins and our future.

Each chapter of this book is dedicated to one of these heroes, who remind us that there's so much more beyond our sky... and yet, there's no place like home.

These celestial objects have helped us to track time and navigate our land and the seas. In some cases, they even make our life on Earth possible. Throughout history, and even to this day, they have been a source of inspiration, sparked our imagination and ignited technological progress that allows us to explore space. They help us to piece together the answers to ancient questions: How did we get here? What happens next? Are we alone in the universe?

Constellations shift, but ancient humans dreamed below the same sky as ours. They created stories to make sense of the world and the mysterious cosmos around them. Knowledge that explains what might seem ordinary today — the Sun rising, the Moon changing — has developed over hundreds of years. But the stories live on and we still tell them today.

While writing this book, I often revisited the initial wonder I felt as a kid when looking at the night skies flooded with stars. I came to realize that it is too easy to take the wonderful sight above for granted.

I hope this book inspires you to head out of your home more often, look up and enjoy the show.
-N.G.

CONTENTS

THE MOON

the HERO OF RHYTHM and RENEWAL

How many times have you looked at the Moon and wondered about it?

Have you noticed how its shape seems to change throughout the month?

Thousands of years ago, humans were looking up and thinking the same thing.

THE MOON
EARTH'S SATELLITE

Earth's long-time companion is the brightest celestial object in the night sky. Even though the Moon remains the same, our view of it is always changing. That is because the Sun lights up different parts of the lunar surface as the Moon goes around the Earth.

THE PHASES OF THE MOON

The different shapes of the Moon that we see throughout a month are called 'phases'.

There are eight phases in the 27 days that it takes the Moon to complete one orbit around Earth. From the southern hemisphere, the illuminated part of the Moon appears on the opposite side.

1. New Moon
The Sun is casting its light on the far side of the Moon. The near side remains dark, so we can't see it.

2. Waxing crescent
From Earth, we can see a crescent shape. 'Waxing' means that it's getting larger.

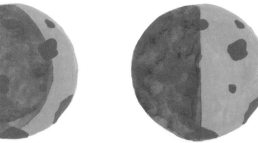

3. First quarter
Half the Moon is visible. It's known as the 'first quarter' because the Moon has travelled a quarter of its journey around Earth.

4. Waxing gibbous
More than half of the Moon is visible, and it's still growing.

5. Full Moon
The near side of the Moon is fully illuminated.

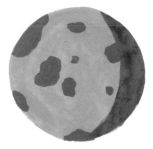

6. Waning gibbous
'Waning' means that the lit area is getting smaller.

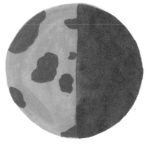

7. Third (last) quarter
Now the opposite side of the Moon is visible.

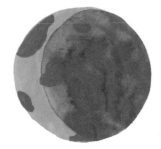

8. Waning crescent
This is the final phase before the new moon.

HIGH AND LOW TIDES

From its moving spot in the sky, the Moon also influences the never-ending cycle of tides on Earth – it makes the water in oceans and seas rise and fall twice every day.

The Moon is Earth's **closest celestial neighbour** – just over 384,000 kilometres away from us. A planet the size of Earth could fit thirty times between us and the Moon.

HOW TO SPOT THE MOON

It takes the same time for the Moon to spin on its axis...

The Moon can be seen from anywhere in the world, almost any time of the year. Its position depends on several things: the time, your location and the Moon's orbit.

Just like the Sun, the Moon rises in the east and sets in the west. This is due to Earth's spin.

But because the Moon has its own motion around our planet, it also slowly moves across the sky, west to east.

This is the reason the Moon doesn't appear in the sky at the same time every night and why sometimes we can see it during the day.

... that it does for it to orbit the Earth.

This is why we always see the same face of the Moon.

FAR SIDE OF THE MOON →

The side of the Moon we can see from Earth is called the 'near side', the side we can't see is the 'far side'.

People have been looking up at the Moon for thousands of years. Observing the lunar cycle, as the Moon passes through its eight phases, was a reliable way of tracking the passage of time – like having a calendar hanging in the sky.

Even with the naked eye, we can see light and dark patches on the Moon. The light areas are known as 'highlands' and the dark ones are called 'maria', meaning 'seas' in Latin. There are no actual seas on the Moon. These dark areas are actually basins that were filled with lava billions of years ago. However, we now know that there is quite a bit of frozen water on the Moon.

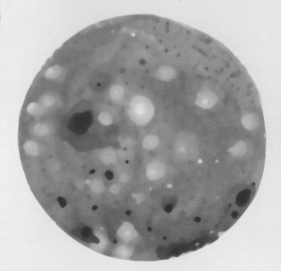

far side

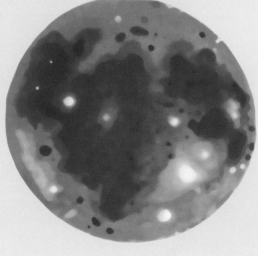

near side

THE MOON: A BRIEF HISTORY

The word 'Moon' comes from the word for month. Jewish, Muslim, Hindu, Chinese, and Celtic cultures, as well as many others, have calendars that count lunar months.

The word for **'month'** and 'Moon' are the same in many Aboriginal Australian languages.

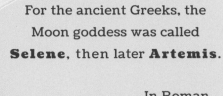

For the ancient Greeks, the Moon goddess was called **Selene**, then later **Artemis**.

In Roman mythology, the Moon was personified as a goddess called **Luna**.

A total of twelve people have walked on the Moon, but the first was American astronaut **Neil Armstrong**, who famously said, 'That's one small step for man; one giant leap for mankind.'

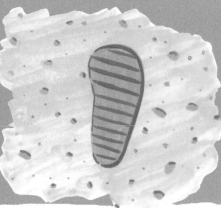

The **Lunar New Year** is a very important holiday in Chinese, Korean, Vietnamese and Malaysian cultures. It is a time of family reunion and takes place on the new moon in early spring each year.

Between 1962 and 1972, NASA (the American space agency) sent several crewed spaceships to the Moon through a space program called **Apollo**. The first human landing on the Moon happened on 20th July, 1969, during the Apollo 11 mission.

In China, people see the companion of the Moon goddess, Chang'e – a **rabbit called Yutu**.

In the northern hemisphere, many people see the **face of a man** on the Moon, inspiring the iconic French film *Le Voyage dans la Lune* by Georges Méliès in 1902.

THE SUN

the HERO OF LIFE and LIGHT

The Sun sets and the night begins. But even when we can't see it, our hero's energy powers our planet through its heat and light. Without the Sun, life on Earth just wouldn't exist.

THE SUN
CENTRE OF THE SOLAR SYSTEM

The Sun is the star at the heart of the Solar System. If Earth is our home, the Solar System is our neighbourhood; we share it with seven planets, some dwarf planets, moons, asteroids, meteoroids and comets. Everything in the Solar System goes around the Sun, while the Sun orbits the centre of our galaxy, the Milky Way.

SOLAR ECLIPSE

A solar eclipse occurs when the **Moon comes between the Earth and the Sun**, getting in the way of the Sun's rays. During the daytime, the shadow of the Moon falls on a portion of the Earth, where the eclipse is visible.

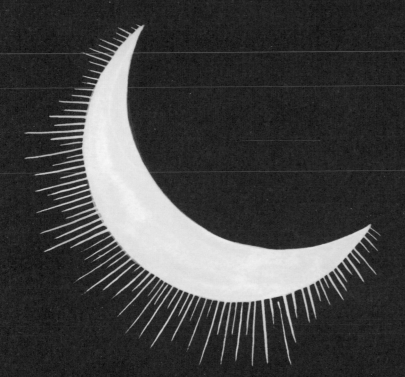

EIGHT MINUTES

The Sun looks so different to the stars we see at night because it's much closer to us. Even so, at around 150 million kilometres away, it still takes sunlight just over 8 minutes to travel from the Sun to Earth!

Be careful watching a solar eclipse. Looking directly at the Sun can damage your eyes forever!

More than a **million Earths** could fit inside the Sun.

The Sun is a huge ball of **really hot gas** (hydrogen and helium). At its core, temperatures reach 15 million degrees Celsius! Luckily for us, Earth is at the perfect distance from it, where life as we know it can thrive.

LUNAR ECLIPSE

A lunar eclipse can only happen during a Full Moon, when the Earth moves in between the Sun and the Moon. We see the Moon slowly become darker as it enters into our planet's shadow – then turn bright again as it exits the shadow.

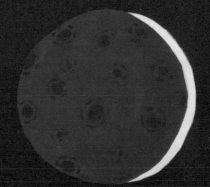

LIGHTS ON!

With its heat and light, the Sun makes it possible for plants and animals to live on Earth.

Sunlight allows plants to make their food through the process of photosynthesis. Using sunlight, carbon dioxide and water, they produce sugars and oxygen – the gas we breathe, and which most life on Earth depends on.

sunlight

carbon dioxide

oxygen

water

The way the Sun interacts with Earth shapes weather and climate. It also powers the water cycle and our star even drives ocean currents by warming the seas.

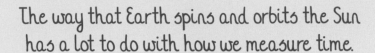
The way that Earth spins and orbits the Sun has a lot to do with how we measure time.

Our planet completes one spin around its axis in twenty-four hours – that's how long a day is.

Earth does one trip around the Sun in about 365 days – that is one year. So even your birthday is relative to how fast we cruise around our star!

BRINGER OF THE SEASONS

The Sun is behind Earth's seasons, which change depending on the position of our planet in relation to the Sun.

When the hemisphere (or half of Earth) where you live is leaning towards the Sun, it's summer there, bringing longer days and warmer weather. The longest day in the northern hemisphere is in June, during the summer solstice.

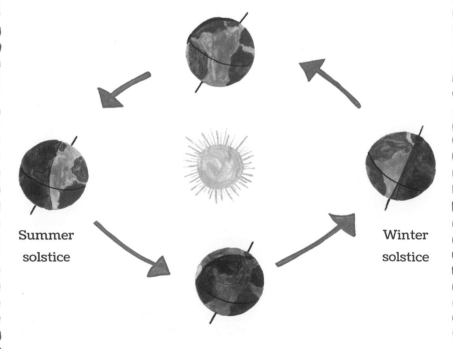

Summer solstice

Winter solstice

The shortest day and the longest night occur in December in the northern hemisphere during the winter solstice, when that hemisphere is fully tilted away from the Sun.

Since ancient times, people have used their observations of the sky to track the passage of time.

The first timekeeping device was the sundial. It used the shadows cast by objects under sunlight to roughly tell the time of day. Sundials from 1500 BCE have been found in Egypt.

Many civilizations created different types of calendars. A solar calendar is based on the time it takes the Earth to complete one orbit around the Sun. The ancient Mayans, who were avid astronomers, created a 365-day solar calendar for their agricultural activities.

THE SUN: A BRIEF HISTORY

The strong influence of the Sun didn't go unnoticed by humans who lived thousands of years before you, and they often considered it a god or a goddess.

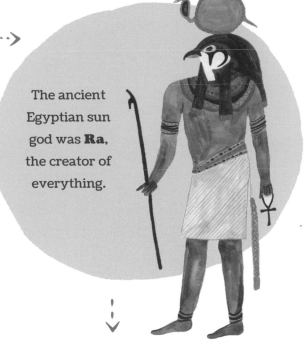

The ancient Egyptian sun god was **Ra**, the creator of everything.

To the **ancient Chinese**, the Sun was the god left out of ten original sun gods. To them, a solar eclipse was caused by a dragon trying to devour the Sun – so they would make noise to frighten the creature away.

In Roman mythology, the sun god is called **Sol**. To this day, the Latin root word *sol* is used to refer to the Sun. That's where the name 'Solar System' comes from!

The Norse sun goddess was also Sól, or **Sunna**, the twin of the moon god, Máni.

Inti was the sun god in the Inca Empire. The most important ceremony was *Inti Raymi*, or 'Sun festival', celebrated during their winter solstice. Today, this traditional ceremony is recreated every year in the ancient city of Cuzco, Peru.

POLARIS

the HERO OF DIRECTION and DEPENDABILITY

Polaris is known as the North Star. For centuries, it has been an important landmark in the night sky, because if you can spot Polaris shining, you know which direction is north.

POLARIS
THE NORTH STAR

Knowing where geographic north – or 'true north' – lies means you can easily work out the rest of the cardinal directions: south, east and west. This is very important information when you are going somewhere, and Polaris, our hero of direction, has been helping humans to find their way for hundreds of years.

HIGHS AND LOWS

The closer you are to the North Pole, the higher in the sky Polaris is. In the North Pole, Polaris appears right above your head! If you are nearer to the equator, Polaris appears closer to the horizon.

FRIEND OF VOYAGERS

Before technology provided us with navigation systems like satnav, voyagers could find their way by observing the night sky – this is called 'celestial navigation'. The North Star is like a reliable compass in the dark night.

Polaris is known as the North Star because it's located really close to a point right above the **North Pole.**

If the skies are free of clouds and dark enough, Polaris **can be seen year-round**.

If you take a compass, keep the 0° edge flat against the horizon and point one arm of the compass at Polaris, the angle you create will tell you your latitude.

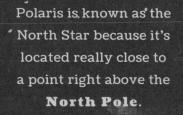

In Old Norse, Polaris was known as *Leidarstjarna,* the **'guiding star'**.

Polaris is only visible in the **northern hemisphere**.

POLE STAR

Polaris is known as a 'fixed star', meaning it doesn't seem to move through the sky like other stars do.

The Earth rotates on its own axis, like a huge spinning top. (The 'axis' is an imaginary line that connects the north celestial pole to the south celestial pole.) It takes one day for Earth to complete one full spin.

This rotation is what makes the Sun and other stars look like they move across the sky – they rise in the east and set in the west. But this doesn't happen to Polaris. Polaris's special location above the North Pole makes it appear stationary in the sky, while the other stars circle around it.

As Earth slowly wobbles on its axis, the position of north in the night sky changes over thousands of years. When the ancient Egyptians were building their pyramids over four millennia ago, a star named Thuban was the North Star. In another 12,000 years from now, that title will belong to a very bright star called Vega.

⚓ MEET THE CONSTELLATION ⚓

Polaris is the brightest star in a constellation called Ursa Minor.

A constellation is a group of stars that form a picture when you draw imaginary lines that connect them. Throughout time, different cultures have created their own constellations, naming and linking them to a unique legend or myth. Ursa Minor, Latin for 'lesser bear' is also known as the Little Bear, because of its shape.

HOW TO SPOT POLARIS

Polaris is the brightest star in Ursa Minor and it is located right at the end of the Little Bear's long tail. Ursa Minor's seven bright stars are commonly known as the Little Dipper. Polaris is at the end of the handle of the Little Dipper.

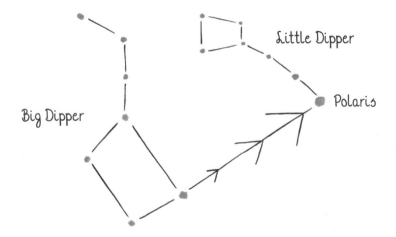

The Little Dipper is not very easy to spot in the night sky, especially when there are a lot of city lights or when the moon is bright. The easiest way to find Polaris is to use the the Plough, which also known as the Big Dipper and is part of the constellation Ursa Major, as a guide. The Big Dipper is easier to find and is also shaped like a ladle. Find the two stars that form the end of its ladle, draw an imaginary line between them, and follow it out until you see Polaris.

As with many of the constellations, there is more than one myth or legend behind Ursa Minor.

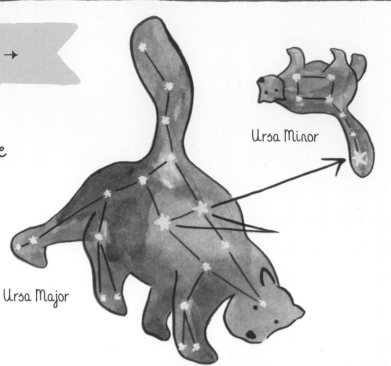

Ursa Minor

Ursa Major

For the ancient Greeks, Ursa Minor represented Arcas. Arcas was the son of Zeus (the king of all the Greek gods) and a female nymph called Callisto. Zeus first transformed Callisto, and then Arcas into bears, and put them in the sky as stars. Callisto is represented by Ursa Major. The two celestial bears remain together.

POLARIS: A BRIEF HISTORY

Polaris has been known by many names, including Pole Star, **Guiding Star** and Lodestar. In Inuit astronomy, Polaris is known as *Nuuttuittuq*, '(the one that) never moves'.

To the Mongols, Polaris was the **peg** holding the world together.

Polaris is not only useful for navigation on Earth. More than 50 years ago, the astronauts of **NASA's Apollo missions** also used the North Star – along with the Sun, Earth and other stars – for orientation on the Moon.

To the ancient Arabs, Polaris was an **evil** star that killed the great warrior of the sky.

In Hawaii, Polaris is known as *Hokupa'a*, which means the **'fixed star'**. Traditional Polynesian sailors used stars like Polaris to navigate the Pacific Ocean in canoes, from Canada to Japan.

Hokupa'a is still used by Hawaiian wayfinders, who memorize the position of the stars to sail the seas.

MERCURY

the HERO OF QUICKNESS and QUIRKINESS

The closest planet to the Sun, Mercury, travels around our star in record time – it is the fastest planet in our Solar System. Its short path around the Sun is quite peculiar, too.

MERCURY
FIRST PLANET FROM THE SUN

Our zippy hero bears extremely high and low temperatures while it speeds around the sun. On Mercury, a year – the time it takes to complete one orbit around the sun – is only 88 Earth days. That's shorter than three Earth months!

LONG DAYS AND SHORT YEARS!

Mercury spins around its own axis very slowly – so slowly, in fact, that one day on Mercury is equal to 59 Earth-days, but a year on Mercury is just 88 Earth-days.

Mercury's orbit is the least circular of all the planets – it's **elliptical**, shaped like an egg. It is sometimes very near the Sun and other times more far away.

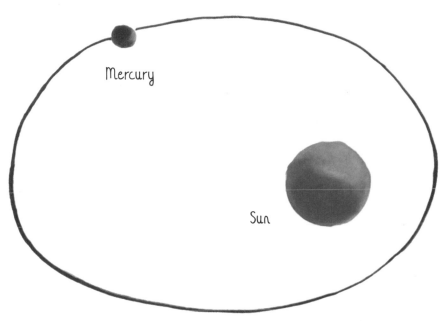

Mercury

Sun

If you were on Mercury when it was closest to the Sun, the star would look **three times bigger** compared to how you see it from Earth!

It can get really **hot and cold** on Mercury, but there's no such thing as summer and winter there. Unlike Earth, Mercury spins on its axis with almost no tilt – so it doesn't experience seasons.

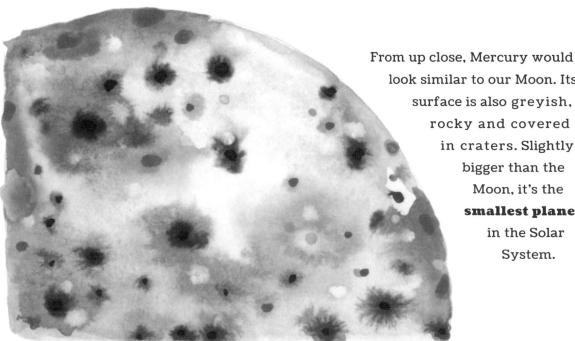

From up close, Mercury would look similar to our Moon. Its surface is also greyish, rocky and covered in craters. Slightly bigger than the Moon, it's the **smallest planet** in the Solar System.

HOT SPOT?

Even though it is the nearest planet to the scorching Sun, Mercury is not the hottest planet in the Solar System. That title goes to Venus, the second closest planet to our host star. Unlike Venus, Mercury doesn't have a thick atmosphere to trap the heat.

SUNRISE, SUNSET →

Because of its unusual orbit, Mercury doesn't have sunrises and sunsets like those we have on Earth.

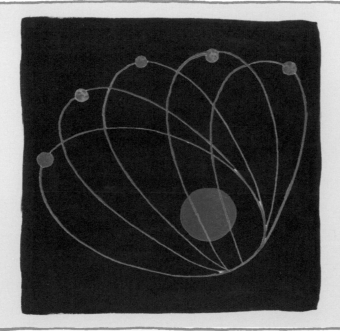

If you were standing on a particular point on Mercury's surface, sometimes you'd notice the Sun rising, then setting, then rising again – all before the end of the day! Then, at sunset, you would see the Sun setting, then rising again before finally setting. This happens because Mercury rotates three times for every two times it completes its egg-shaped orbit of the sun.

MERCURY IN RETROGRADE →

Three to four times a year, observers on Earth can catch Mercury crossing the sky 'in reverse' – that is, from west to east, instead of the usual east to west.

But this doesn't mean that Mercury suddenly starts to move backwards! Astronomers call this 'retrograde motion' and it's just an illusion caused by the way that Earth and Mercury move in their own orbits. This happens with the rest of the planets we can see with the naked eye, too: Venus, Mars, Jupiter and Saturn.

HOW TO SPOT MERCURY

Mercury is one of the most elusive planets seen from Earth. When and where to spot Mercury depends on different factors, such as its location in its orbit, or where you live. In the evening, you can try finding the direction of sunset, then searching not very high above the horizon as soon as the Sun disappears.

The sky is never fully dark when Mercury makes its appearance. Because its orbit lies between Earth and the Sun, sometimes you can spot the small planet glowing right after sunset and at other times it appears before sunrise, but you won't catch it in the middle of the night.

Thirteen times each century, Mercury can be observed passing between the Earth and the Sun! This rare astronomical event is called a 'transit'. When it happens, we can see the planet's tiny silhouette like a moving dot against the sun. The next transit of Mercury will be in 2032.

MYSTERIOUS MERCURY

Our mysterious hero is one of the least-explored planets in our Solar System.

Travelling to Mercury means getting close to the Sun, so it's not easy to study it up close. Its surface remains unexplored, as no lander has ever descended on it – at least not yet.

Only two spacecraft have visited Mercury in the past: Mariner 10 took images of almost half of the surface in the 1970s; MESSENGER orbited the planet for four years until 2015. But we might discover a lot more about Mercury with the BepiColombo mission, which is due to enter the planet's orbit in late 2025 to study it in depth.

Unveiling the secrets of Mercury will help scientists better understand how planets like it were born.

MERCURY: A BRIEF HISTORY

Ancient Greeks named the speedy planet after their fastest god, **Hermes**. Often wearing a helmet with wings, he was the quick messenger for all the gods.

In Roman mythology, the equivalent of Hermes is the god **Mercury** – the name the planet is known by in Western cultures.

Mercury was first viewed with a telescope about four centuries ago by British astronomer **Thomas Harriot** and Italian scientist **Galileo Galilei**.

In Germanic mythology, the planet was associated with the god **Woden**, or Odin, after whom the day of the week, **Wednesday,** is named.

In ancient China, Mercury was *Chen Xing*, **'the hour star'**, linked to the water element. In modern Chinese, Korean, Vietnamese and Japanese cultures, the planet is known as **'the water star'**.

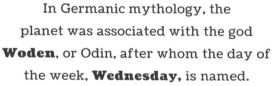

In Hindu mythology, Mercury was named after the god **Budha**, protector of merchants.

ORION'S BELT

the HERO OF TALES and TRIOS

Three bright, blue-white stars form the belt of a giant figure in the night sky...

Orion: one of the most familiar shapes to stargazers from all over the world.

Orion's Belt is an asterism, or pattern of three stars, within the popular constellation of Orion. Orion is commonly known as the Hunter, based on the Greek myth. It depicts the figure of an enormous man in the sky who looks like he is wearing a belt.

TRIO OF STARS

Orion's Belt is one of the many names for the trio of stars that line up as a belt. Collectively, they're also known as the Weighing Beam, Frigg's Distaff and Three Sisters, among other names. They are roughly the same age and may have originated in the same nebula.

Betelgeuse

Alnitak is actually a system of three stars, thousands of times brighter than our Sun, which appear as one to the naked eye.

Mintaka also comes from an Arabic word meaning 'belt'.

Alnilam is the central star in Orion's Belt. The name means 'string of pearls' in Arabic.

BURNING BRIGHT

The stars that give shape to the Hunter are among the most luminous in the whole sky. **Rigel** is seventh on the list – and it's also the brightest star in the Orion constellation. This blue supergiant marks Orion's western knee. **Betelgeuse**, his western shoulder, is a red supergiant, and is the sky's tenth most luminous star.

Rigel

The constellation rises in the east and sets in the west, and it goes high in the sky during the night. The easiest way to find Orion is by locating its belt. Look for three stars that are roughly evenly spaced and form a short, straight line.

You can use the celestial Hunter to find Sirius (the Dog Star), which lies to the lower left of the belt, and The Pleiades star cluster (also called 'The Seven Sisters'), which can be found to the upper-right of the constellation.

Around 21st October every year, the constellation seems to offer a spectacle: the Orionids meteor shower. Thousands of space rocks light up as they penetrate Earth's atmosphere, radiating from Orion.

If you live in the northern half of the world, then Orion's constellation will be visible during the winter. If you are stargazing from the southern hemisphere, then you'll find Orion shining bright during the summer.

AN ANCIENT SHAPE

Thousands of years ago, people gazed up and saw Orion's Belt – and it looked almost exactly as it does right now. This is not always the case: many other asterisms and constellations seem to drift apart over millennia. But Orion's Belt has remained consistent throughout humankind's history.

This is because the three stars that form the belt originated in the same place. And, what's more, they have been travelling in the same direction all this time! So, even though they are several light-years apart from each other (and although they are really far away from Earth), they remain together in the night sky as we see it.

ORION'S BELT: A BRIEF HISTORY

In the Western world, Orion's Belt is sometimes called The **Three Kings** (*Reyes Magos* in Spanish) in connection to the three wise men or Magi from the Bible.

A NEVER-ENDING HUNT →

Since ancient times, several stories have explained how Orion came to be.

In Greek mythology, the constellation is associated with Orion, a hunter carrying a hunting tool and wearing a belt.

There is more than one version of the Greek myth. In most of them, Orion was a hunter who was stung by a scorpion (represented in the sky by the constellation Scorpius). Feeling sorry for the hunter and his tragic death, the gods put Orion in the heavens. But they didn't leave him there alone: they also placed his beloved dogs, in the form of the constellations Canis Major and Canis Minor.

Orion

Canis Minor

Canis Major

Lepus

Taurus

The myth says the gods also made sure Orion had celestial animals to hunt – a hare (Lepus) and a bull (Taurus).

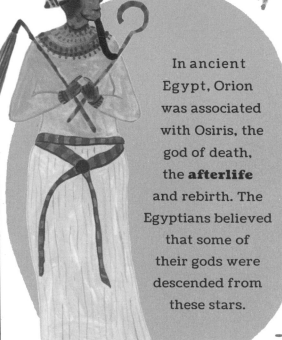

In ancient Egypt, Orion was associated with Osiris, the god of death, the **afterlife** and rebirth. The Egyptians believed that some of their gods were descended from these stars.

For the Tswana people (from South Africa and Botswana), the stars in Orion's Belt represent three **warthogs** who are being chased by three dogs. The dogs are associated with the stars that form Orion's sword, known as *dintsa le Dikolobe*.

Spanish-speaking people in Latin America call the three stars in Orion's Belt *Las Tres Marías*. In Brazil, they are called As *Três Marias* (in Portuguese). Both names mean 'The **Three Marys**'.

VENUS

the HERO OF BEGINNINGS *and* ENDINGS

Venus is known as our 'Morning Star' or 'Evening Star' – even though it is, in fact, a planet.

When viewed from Earth, Venus makes quite an entrance in our sky by glowing steadily around sunrise or sunset.

VENUS
EARTH'S TWIN

Venus is the brightest object in the night sky after the Moon. Ancient cultures believed our hero to be two stars – one that shined bright at the beginning of the day, and another that appeared as the day was ending. Now we know that this planet glows in the morning or in the evening, depending on its position on its path around the Sun.

Venus is the second planet from the Sun – and is sometimes called '**Earth's twin**' because it has a similar size and interior structure, with a rocky crust, a mantle and a metal core.

Venus orbits the Sun faster than our planet, so years on Venus are shorter – about 225 Earth days. However, Venus rotates on its axis really slowly – **one day lasts 243 Earth days**. This means that on Venus, the years are shorter than the days!

While Earth hosts abundant life, Venus is a **hostile world** – it is full of volcanoes, wrapped in toxic clouds, subjected to powerful winds, and is extremely hot.

Because the days are so long, the sun rises just twice a year on Venus. In other words, **sunrise** only happens every four Earth months!

From Venus's sky, the Sun rises in the west and sets in the east – the opposite of what we observe from Earth. This is because Venus **spins backwards** compared to other planets.

Walking on Venus would be impossible – you would get crushed against the ground! The planet's **air pressure** is many times that of Earth.

FEMALE TOUCH

All but three geological places on Venus are named after women. Craters are given the names of famous women, or just any female first name. Mountains are named after goddesses.

The clouds in Venus's sky are nothing like the cotton-wool clouds we have on Earth. Venus is covered by a blanket of thick, yellowish cloud made of sulphuric acid, a toxic chemical that smells like rotten eggs!

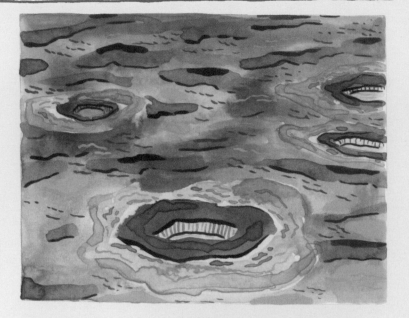

These clouds, plus an atmosphere filled with carbon dioxide, don't let the heat escape. This is known as the greenhouse effect – when the Sun's energy passes through the atmosphere and warms up the planet's surface, but then the atmosphere doesn't let the heat leave… and the planet gets even hotter.

Scientists believe that millions of years ago, Venus could have had oceans of liquid water like Earth. But because of the greenhouse effect, the water turned into vapour. Learning about Venus's history can tell us what could happen in Earth's future.

HOW TO SPOT VENUS

After the Moon, Venus is the brightest natural object in the night sky. Because of its thick cover of toxic clouds, the planet reflects a lot of light from the Sun. That's why you can also see Venus during the daytime.

Our hero is pretty near to the Sun, so from Earth, we always see the two of them fairly close to each other. That means Venus is usually quite easy to find! Just look for it right after sunset (facing west) or around sunrise (in the east). Enjoy its steady light for a few hours.

Venus is not always visible, though. Sometimes it hides behind the sun. Other times, Venus appears so close to the sun it is difficult to see.

before sunrise

sunrise

after sunrise

♀
VENUS: A BRIEF HISTORY
♀

We have known about our brilliant hero for thousands of years, since you don't need a telescope to see it.

Venus is the only planet named after a **female**. In Roman mythology, Venus is the goddess of love and beauty. Italian painter Botticelli showed her standing on a huge scallop shell.

MEET THE PLANET

Because it is so close to Earth, our hero has been studied quite a lot through the years.

Venus was the first planet ever to be explored by a spacecraft! NASA's Mariner 2 flew by Venus in December, 1962. Ever since, humans have sent multiple spacecrafts to study the scorching world.

The first planetary surface to be touched by a spacecraft from Earth belonged to Venus! The Soviet Union sent several probes and landers called Venera in the 1960s and 1970s. Because of the boiling environment and crushing pressure, though they didn't survive for long.

In 2005, the European Space Agency launched the Venus Express that orbited the planet for more than eight years – and discovered the its peculiar lightning. Japan's probe Akatsuki began orbiting Venus in 2015.

More missions to explore Venus up close are scheduled for the future. So we will learn much more about our hero in the next few years!

Ancient Sumerians associated Venus with **Inanna**, goddess of love and war.

The Lakota people named the planet Aŋpo Wiŋ, or the **'Light of Dawn'**.

Ancient Maya called Venus **Ahzab Kab Ek**, 'the star that awakens the Earth'.

In some languages, Venus has a name meaning **'daystar'**.

In Slavic mythology, many know the planet as **Danica** – the younger sister of the Sun.

HALLEY'S COMET

the HERO
OF WONDER
and WARINESS

Ready to make a wish? This celestial visitor
can be seen from Earth only every 75 years.
But each year, we get two meteor showers
that remind us of its future return!

HALLEY'S COMET
1P/HALLEY

Ask a grown-up if they remember the night sky of 1986. This was the last chance the world had to view the most famous comet of all - Halley's Comet. Viewing conditions weren't ideal in 1986, but they are set to be better the next time, which is predicted to be in 2061!

DIRTY SNOWBALL

A comet is made of ice, dust, frozen gases and rock (it's been called a 'dirty snowball'). Comets are leftovers from when the Solar System formed 4.6 billion years ago, so they hold clues to our past.

When comets get closer to the Sun, they heat up. The gases and dust from the core gush out and form a glowing head, called a **'coma'**. The solar wind blows the material into two brilliant tails that can extend for millions of kilometres.

The world has observed Halley's Comet for thousands of years – but only in 1705 did astronomer **Edmund Halley** realize that it was the same comet coming back every 75 years! The famous comet is named in his honour.

Many millions of comets share the Solar System with us. Some, like Halley's Comet, live in a region called the **Kuiper Belt** – it's a disc that extends from the orbit of Neptune, the furthest planet from the Sun.

Scientists even think that comets might have a lot to do with **life on Earth**. By crashing into our planet ages past, they might have brought water and organic material – basic ingredients that make life possible.

FROZEN HEART

When they're far away from the Sun, comets are just a frozen core that can be many kilometres wide.

Halley's Comet measures 15 x 8 kilometres – as large as a small town! Its core is potato-shaped.

IS HALLEY'S COMET REALLY A COMET?

It's easy to confuse similar-looking celestial objects! Here's a guide:

COMET

Halley's Comet *is* a comet! Comets are made of ice and dust. They orbit the Sun and, when they come close to it, they develop a head and a tail.

ASTEROID

Asteroids are rocky objects that also orbit the Sun. They come in different shapes and sizes, but they are much smaller than a planet.

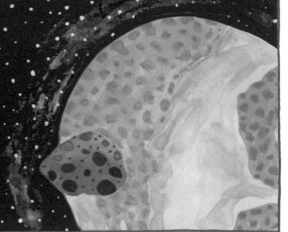

METEOROID

Meteoroids are typically small: as small as a fleck of dust to the size of a boulder. They are the result of two asteroids crashing, or they are shed from comets.

METEOR ('SHOOTING STAR')

When meteoroids enter Earth's atmosphere, they become meteors. The friction with the air causes them to burn up. The streaks of light they leave in the sky are what we call shooting stars. When our planet comes across many meteoroids at once, a meteor shower happens.

METEORITE

When a meteor is able to enter our atmosphere without vaporizing completely, and lands somewhere on Earth, it becomes a meteorite.

IT'S RAINING SHOOTING STARS!

As Halley's Comet travels in space, it disintegrates a little and leaves behind a stream of space debris or 'meteoroids'. Every year, Earth moves through this debris trail. This causes a brief, spectacular celestial show: a meteor shower!

The different meteor showers happen annually at around the same time, when many meteors seem to radiate from the same part of the sky. Halley's Comet is responsible for two meteor showers: the Eta Aquariids in May and the Orionids in October.

Meteors, or 'shooting stars', can be observed with the naked eye – you just need a clear sky. So look up and enjoy the show!

MARK THESE IN YOUR CALENDAR →

Quadrantids: December/January

Lyrids: April

Eta Aquariids: May

Perseids: August (usually, the most visible meteor shower of the year; it's caused by debris from the tail of a comet called Swift-Tuttle).

Orionids: October

Leonids: November

Geminids: December

Because Halley's Comet's visits are predictable, scientists were ready for it the last time our hero came close to Earth in 1986.

As the comet's 1986 return approaached, many countries teamed up to send spacecrafts to observe the ancient visitor from space. The collaboration was called Halley Watch.

Giotto, a probe sent by the European Space Agency, was able to take a close look at the comet's nucleus. The images it sent back to Earth helped us better understand Halley's Comet and comets in general.

Halley's Comet was the first one to be imaged by an interplanetary spacecraft. Since then, other missions have closely examined different comets. Some robotic probes have even landed on comets, and others have brought samples to Earth, so scientists can study them here!

HALLEY'S COMET: A BRIEF HISTORY

Through the ages, comets have been observed with both wonder and fear. For some ancient people, Halley's Comet was a **bad sign** – they linked the cosmic traveller to death and destruction.

The earliest record of Halley's appearance was made in ancient China. Our hero was described as a '**broom star**', seen in the sky around 240 B.C. Chinese astronomers documented comets' visits over centuries – very useful information for later stargazers.

When Halley's Comet visited in 1066, people in England thought it would bring misfortune. Then, the Anglo-Saxon, Harold Godwinson, was killed at the Battle of Hastings. This episode – along with the comet – was later depicted in the **Bayeux Tapestry**.

Why do we wish upon a shooting star? The ancient astronomer **Ptolemy** believed that meteors were a sign of the gods gazing at humans and listening to their wishes.

MARS

the HERO OF INVESTIGATION and IMAGINATION

After Earth, Mars is the planet we've explored the most. Our hero's reddish glow in the night sky is a constant reminder of humans' search for life beyond our blue world.

MARS
THE RED PLANET

For many years, people suspected that Mars was populated by aliens. We now know this is not the case, but to this day, scientists continue the search for signs of past Martian life. Spacecrafts and robotic explorers are hard at work studying the rocky, dusty world. In the future, human explorers could travel there, too.

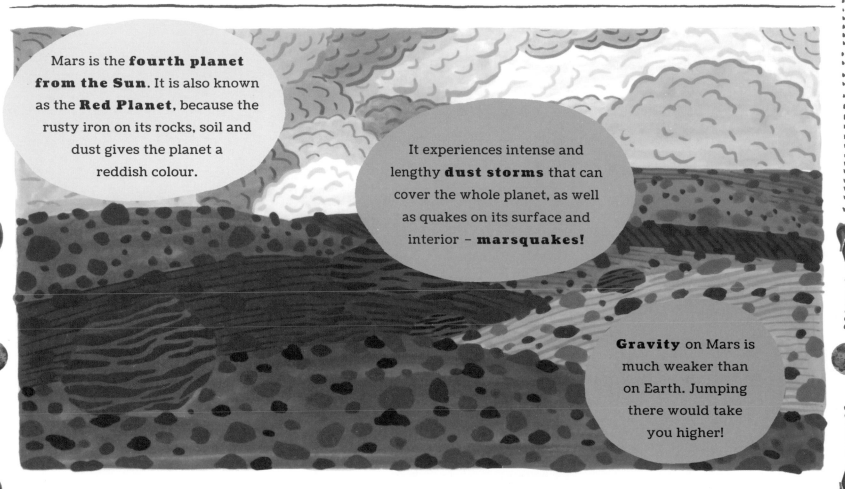

Mars is the **fourth planet from the Sun**. It is also known as the **Red Planet**, because the rusty iron on its rocks, soil and dust gives the planet a reddish colour.

It experiences intense and lengthy **dust storms** that can cover the whole planet, as well as quakes on its surface and interior – **marsquakes!**

Gravity on Mars is much weaker than on Earth. Jumping there would take you higher!

Mars is a cold, terrestrial world with **deserts**, inactive **volcanoes** and polar **ice caps**.

The Martian atmosphere is about a hundred times thinner than Earth's. And humans wouldn't be able to breathe the air because it has very little **oxygen**.

TWO MOONS

Mars is not alone in outer space. Two small moons, called Phobos and Deimos, orbit the planet. Instead of looking round like our Moon, Phobos is shaped like potatoes!

♂

OLYMPUS MONS

Mars is home to the tallest mountain and the largest known canyon in the Solar System. Olympus Mons is almost 2.5 times the height of Mount Everest. Valles Marineris, 'the Grand Canyon of Mars', stretches over 4,000 kilometres across the Red Planet.

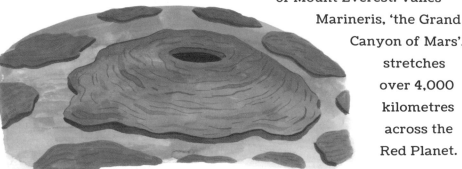

HOW TO SPOT MARS

Mars is visible to the naked eye.

Our hero is actually quite easy to spot. Just look for a glowing orange-red dot in the night sky, almost all year round.

In fact, from Earth, five planets are visible to the naked eye: Mercury, Venus, Mars, Jupiter and Saturn. They all shine with different colours!

To determine if you are looking at a star or a planet, check if it twinkles. Stars twinkle, but planets don't. This is because planets are much closer to us than stars.

And if you look at the planets through a telescope, their different colours reveal themselves clearly...

MEET THE PLANET

No astronaut has set foot on Martian soil yet, but Mars is the planet humans have explored most.

NASA's *Mariner 4* passed by the mysterious world in 1965, while several other countries have sent spacecrafts to orbit Mars, to collect information. The first spacecrafts to touch the Martian surface were NASA's *Viking Landers*, which arrived in 1976.

Several robots have visited Mars, too! These are called 'rovers' – they receive orders from engineers on Earth and study the soil, the rocks, the weather and the air on Mars. The first one, *Sojourner*, landed in 1997. The most recent rovers exploring the Red Planet are *Curiosity* and *Perseverance*, sent by NASA, and *Zhurong*, sent by China. In 2021, a helicopter that launched attached to *Perseverance's* belly became the first aircraft to fly in another planet!

Saturn
golden, brown and blue-grey

Mercury
grey

Venus
yellow

Mars
red, brown and tan

Jupiter
brown, orange and tan, with white cloud stripes

LIFE ON MARS →

In ages past, Mars might have been a watery world, just like Earth.

There are signs of long-gone rivers and lakes as well as massive floods. The now-dry planet might have had a thicker atmosphere millions of years ago. Now, liquid water can't exist for long on the surface because it evaporates quickly.

There is still water on Mars, though. It can be found in the form of ice (mixed with dust) under the surface in the poles. Water is also present in thin clouds. At times, liquid salty water might flow down some hillsides and craters.

All the forms of life that we know about need water to exist. Scientists are looking for evidence to answer very intriguing questions: Was there ever life on Mars? And could Mars host life in the future?

MARS: A BRIEF HISTORY

The ancient Romans named Mars after their **god of war**. The planet's distinct colour reminded them of blood.

In Greek mythology, the counterpart of Mars as the god of war is called **Ares**. The planet's moons, Phobos and Deimos, get their names from two of the horses that pulled Ares's chariot. Phobos means 'fear'; Deimos means 'terror'.

In ancient Babylon, the planet was named after **Nergal**, while in Hindu texts, it is known as **Angaraka** – both gods of fire and war.

In ancient Chinese mythology, Mars was known as the '**fire star**', a warning of death and destruction to come.

Sometimes Mars appears to go backwards in the sky then forward again in a circular movement. This is an optical illusion; it happens because Earth travels faster than Mars. The Ininew, one of Canada's largest First Nations groups, call this *mooswa acak*: '**moose spirit**'. This is because of how a moose moves when it's startled.

The idea of aliens on Mars has sparked artists' imaginations for centuries. Over a hundred years ago, the English author **H. G. Wells** wrote the science-fiction novel *The War of the Worlds*, which was about a Martian invasion.

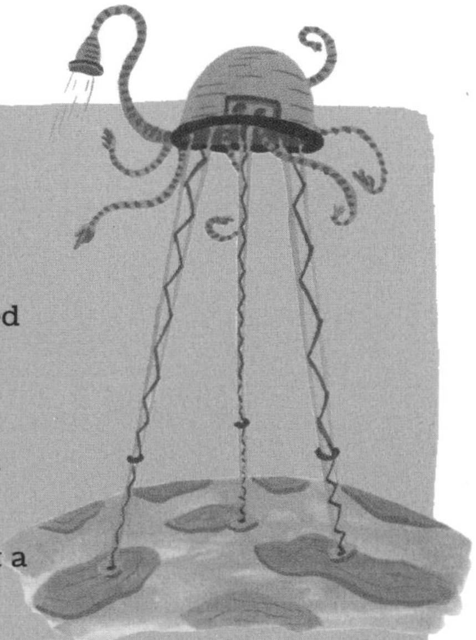

Our hero has inspired songs, too. The famous English singer and songwriter **David Bowie** performed many songs about space – one of them was 'Life on Mars?'

ALIOTH

the HERO OF NATURE *and* NAVIGATION

Alioth is the brightest star in the popular constellation Ursa Major, the 'Great Bear' - you can find Alioth in the bear's tail.

Throughout history, this brilliant star has helped voyagers to find their way.

ALIOTH
EPSILON URSAE MAJORIS

Because it's so brilliant and easy to find, our hero is one of the 58 navigational stars – and the brightest one in the constellation Ursa Major. People use Alioth to navigate Earth... and the night sky!: The Plough is used to find other stars and constellations, including the Little Dipper, Ursa Minor and the stars Polaris, Arcturus and Spica.

Alioth is about **83 light-years** from Earth, while our star, the Sun, is just over 8 light-minutes away.

It is bigger, more massive and younger than our Sun. And it's around **102 times brighter**, too!

Alioth

The Plough

Alioth is part of a landmark in the sky: the **Plough**, found within Ursa Major.

THE PLOUGH

Within Ursa Major is the asterism the Plough (also called the Big Dipper), whose shape is the most recognizable of all the those in the constellation.

Throughout different cultures, the Plough is associated with many shapes: from a cart or wagon, to a salmon net, a saucepan and a coffin.

TRAVELLING THROUGH SPACE

All stars travel across space – just like us on Earth, but they are so far away that you wouldn't notice. Alioth is part of an association of stars called the Ursa Major Moving Group. Astronomers believe that these stars all formed in the same place around 300 million years ago – and that they travel in space at similar speeds.

Ursa Major, home of our hero Alioth, takes up a large portion of the sky.

This constellation not only helps travellers to find their way around on Earth – astronomers also use it to navigate the skies.

In the region of space where you see Ursa Major, there also are many deep space objects like whole galaxies! The Pinwheel Galaxy and the Sunflower Galaxy are some of them.

Pinwheel Galaxy

Sunflower Galaxy

HOW TO SPOT ALIOTH

Alioth, and the pattern of stars that make up the Plough, are only visible in the northern hemisphere. Spotting Alioth in the night sky should be easy. To locate it, find the Plough first – it's a pattern of seven stars that look like a huge spoon for serving soup. Once you spot it, find the third star of the Plough's handle, closer to the bowl – that's Alioth.

During the spring, you can find the Plough high in the night sky. In the autumn, it will appear closer to the horizon, but it never disappears. That's because the Plough is circumpolar in most of the northern half of the world. Due to the Earth's rotation, the large cosmic spoon looks like it slowly rotates around the north celestial pole in an anticlockwise motion.

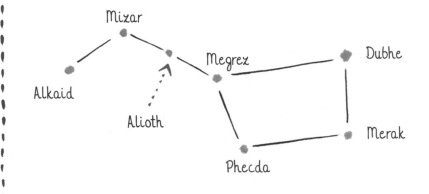

There's also the Owl Nebula, a region of space full of cosmic gases and dust – leftovers of a dying star. When seen using larger telescopes, this nebula looks like the eyes of a celestial owl.

Owl Nebula

ALIOTH: A BRIEF HISTORY

The asterism that contains Alioth was often associated with **agricultural** themes. In the United Kingdom, the asterism became known as the Plough, while the Irish name is *An Camchéachta*, meaning 'the bent plough'.

In Latin, the seven stars that make up the Plough were known as the *septentriones*, meaning the '**seven oxen**'.

The Plough had an important role in the **Underground Railroad** – a network of places, routes and people in the U.S. that helped enslaved black people from the south to find freedom in the north. Because it was safer to travel at night, those who escaped used the Plough to find Polaris, which showed them the way north. Folk songs said to 'Follow the Drinking Gourd' (Plough) towards freedom.

Some Native American groups, such as the Iroquois, see the stars that form the Plough as a **bear**. The stars in the handle are brave hunters, forever chasing the creature across the sky. The wounded bear's blood turns the leaves red in autumn.

In **Arabian mythology**, the Plough represents a funeral. The bowl shape is the coffin, and the three stars that form the handle – including Alioth – are the mourners that follow behind it.

The **Alaskan state flag** features the Plough and the North Star against a dark-blue background. The flag was designed by Benny Benson, a 13 year-old boy! He chose it because the Great Bear (Ursa Major) symbolizes strength.

Throughout Europe, the Plough is known by different names. In German, it is known as *Großer Wagen*: '**Great Cart**'. In Finnish, it is referred to as *Otava*: '**Salmon Net**'.

JUPITER

the HERO OF MAJESTY and MAGNITUDE

Jupiter is a giant within our Solar System. All the planets in the Solar System could easily fit inside it - twice! Our hero is an enormous and colourful ball of gases, where powerful winds blow non-stop.

JUPITER
THE GAS GIANT

The fifth planet from the Sun, Jupiter is the largest planet in our galactic neighbourhood. It is one of the 'gas giants' – gigantic planets with no solid surface to walk on. White and reddish bands of clouds wrap around it, punctuated by its iconic Great Red Spot.

Despite being huge, Jupiter **spins really fast** – one day on Jupiter lasts less than 10 hours.

Our hero is five times further away from the Sun than Earth. That means it takes sunlight **43 minutes** to reach Jupiter!

GREAT RED SPOT

Our hero is a turbulent world, covered in a thick and cloudy atmosphere. If you looked at Jupiter through a telescope, you'd see a huge, swirling patch. That is the Great Red Spot, a massive storm twice as wide as Earth. It has been blowing for at least three hundred years!

Europa

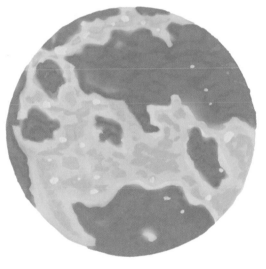

Ganymede

Jupiter has at least **79 moons**. The four largest are called Io, Ganymede, Callisto and Europa.

Io

Three of these large moons have an **icy crust**, but they may have vast oceans of liquid water under the surface. This is exciting – it means they could potentially support life.

Callisto

Temperatures in Jupiter's clouds can reach around **-145 degrees Celsius**, but the planet gets extremely hot near its centre.

KING OF THE SOLAR SYSTEM

Jupiter is an absolutely huge planet and very distinctive to look at, with its stripes and iconic red spot.

It is composed mostly of hydrogen and helium (just like our Sun), so it could have been a star. However, Jupiter didn't grow massive enough, so it never started burning.

Jupiter is the first of the 'outer planets' of the Solar System, counting outwards from the Sun. The 'inner planets' are rocky worlds: Mercury, Venus, Earth and Mars. The 'outer planets' are the gas giants Jupiter and Saturn, and the icy worlds Uranus and Neptune.

Mercury   Venus   Earth   Mars   Jupiter   Saturn   Uranus   Neptune

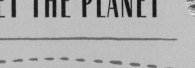 MEET THE PLANET

Over four centuries ago, the Italian astronomer Galileo Galilei observed Jupiter through a telescope for the first time, discovering its four largest moons.

Juno

The first missions to observe Jupiter up close were the Pioneer and Voyager probes in the 1970s. In 1995, the Galileo spacecraft began to study the planet in-depth. In the twenty-first Century, the Cassini and New Horizons missions also took a look at our hero (on their way to their final destinations).

Most recently, the Juno mission was launched specifically to study Jupiter and its largest moons. The spacecraft has been sharing high-resolution images and data... Not an easy task, since Jupiter is the most radioactive planet in the Solar System!

In the near future, the Europa Clipper and Jupiter Ice Moons Explorer missions will look at Jupiter's fascinating icy moons.

HOW TO SPOT JUPITER

You can observe Jupiter's bright, steady, white light without binoculars or a telescope from anywhere in the world. It is usually the second-brightest planet in the night sky after Venus. It is even more brilliant than Sirius, the most luminous star in the night sky. When Jupiter passes closest to our planet (every 13 months or so) it appears even brighter to us, but when it moves too near to the Sun it becomes impossible to see it from Earth. Don't worry, it will be back again soon!

JUPITER: A BRIEF HISTORY

The ancient Romans named Jupiter, the largest planet, after the king of all their gods. Jupiter was associated with **thunder and lightning**. He ruled the skies.

Hindu astrologers knew the planet as **Guru**, meaning 'teacher'. They associated it with wisdom and learning.

In Germanic and Norse mythology, Jupiter is associated with **Thor**, god of the sky, thunder and lightning, and son of Odin, king of the gods.

In China, Vietnam, Japan and Korea, Jupiter is known as the 'wood star'. The name is based on the Chinese **Five Elements**, a philosophy that sees the world in constant change.

The Babylonians knew Jupiter as **Marduk**, a god and protector of the city of Babylon (within modern-day Iraq). This ancient civilization used geometry to track the movements of Jupiter across the heavens.

SIRIUS

the HERO OF LUSTRE *and* LOYALTY

Sirius is the brightest star in our dark, velveteen sky.

Its unmistakable glow stands out in the constellation of Canis Major, Latin for 'Greater Dog' – that's why its nickname is the 'Dog Star'.

SIRIUS
THE DOG STAR

The brightest star in the night sky is about twice as massive as the Sun and 25 times more intense! But our celestial hero looks smaller and dimmer than the Sun because it is almost nine light-years away. The name 'Sirius' comes from the Greek word *seirios*, meaning 'glowing'.

DOG DAYS

Have you ever heard the expression 'dog days'?. In the northern hemisphere, people in ancient times believed that the hottest days of the summer were caused by the Dog Star being close to the Sun in our daytime sky.

Like all stars, Sirius moves through space – and it's **getting closer** to our Solar System. This means it will look even brighter to us in the distant future.

Sirius has a companion in space – another star! When you gaze at Sirius, you are actually looking at **two stars** that orbit each other – Sirius A and Sirius B. Many of the stars we observe at night are a **'binary system'** like this.

UFO

Our hero changes colour while it flickers, especially when it's near the horizon. This has led people to report it as an **Unidentified Flying Object**!

Sirius A

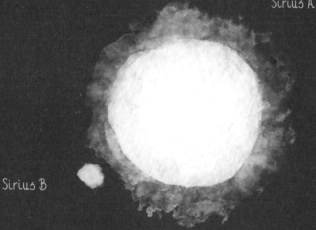

Sirius B

With the naked eye, you can see Sirius A, which is much larger and brighter than its companion, Sirius B. Sirius B is the dim core of a dead star – a **white dwarf**.

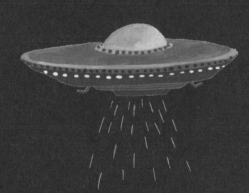

Sirius's actual colour doesn't change, though. We see it that way because Earth's atmosphere affects starlight when it passes through it.

Every star you see in the sky was born mostly from a gas called hydrogen together with clouds of dust. The individual clouds are named 'nebula'.

First, a nebula collapses and form a hot core, called a 'protostar'. The protostar gets hotter and hotter until eventually it starts to create a gas called helium. This generates heat and energy – and the star begins to shine!

Some stars are hotter, larger, or brighter than others. But they all meet the same fate: when they run out of fuel, they die.

Stars that are not quite so massive expel their material into space, leaving just the hot core and becoming a white dwarf – like Sirius B.

Stars with greater mass die with an enormous explosion called a 'supernova', which may create an incredibly dense object: a neutron star. The most massive stars die by collapsing into themselves, leaving behind a very mysterious object: a black hole.

DOGS IN THE SKY

Sirius's home in our sky is in Canis Major, a constellation in the southern hemisphere.

HOW TO SPOT SIRIUS

First, locate Orion's Belt. The three stars of the belt point towards Sirius, which is located to the bottom-left at a distance about eight times the width of the belt. The star they point to has a distinct blue-white colour, and is the most brilliant of all its neighbours.

When Sirius is closer to the horizon, you might notice that it flashes in different colours. This is because its light is passing through a thicker part of Earth's atmosphere.

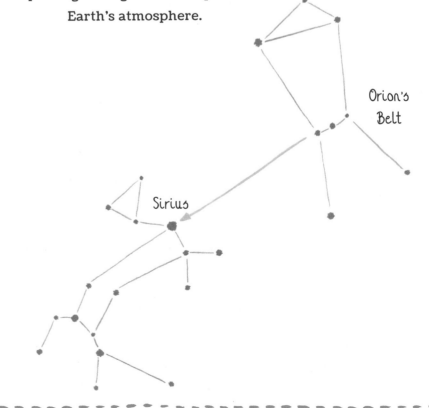

Orion's Belt

Sirius

In Greek mythology, Canis Major represents the larger of the two dogs that follow the constellation of Orion, the Hunter.

Orion's loyal dog can be seen chasing a hare, represented by a dimmer constellation known as Lepus. The smaller hunting dog next to Orion is Canis Minor, or the 'lesser dog'.

The constellation was associated with another Greek myth, in which Canis Major represented Laelaps, a hunting dog destined to always catch its prey.

Zeus, the chief of all the Olympian gods, gifted Laelaps to a princess named Europa. Eventually, Laelaps was given an impossible task: to hunt the Teumessian Fox, a creature that was fated never to be caught. The chase continued until Zeus decided to put both animals in the night sky for eternity.

SIRIUS: A BRIEF HISTORY

To the ancient Polynesians, the star was the body of the 'Great Bird' constellation, **Manu**, which was important for navigating the seas, as it divided the sky into two halves.

To the Māori, Sirius is known as **Takurua** and is associated with the beginning of winter.

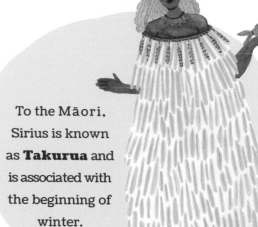

In India, Sirius is associated with **Svana**, the loyal dog of Prince Yudhisthira. During a search to find heaven, the prince's siblings abandoned him, but the dog stayed. When Yudhisthira and his canine companion finally arrived at the gates of heaven, they were both allowed through.

In ancient Egypt, it was called the **Nile Star** and was associated with gods such as Osiris and Sopdet. After several weeks out of view, it appeared right before the rise of the Nile River which nourished the lands.

Ancient Greeks linked Sirius's presence in the sky with the **hottest days** of the year. Its twinkling was seen as a bad influence and was thought to bring on fevers.

SATELLITES

the HEROES OF COMMUNICATION *and* COOPERATION

Thousands of artificial satellites orbiting our planet bring countless benefits to life on Earth...

And the biggest of them all is the International Space Station.

SATELLITES
EARTH'S ORBITERS

Satellites are objects that orbit another body – they can be a moon, a planet, an asteroid or a star. Even Earth is a satellite going around the Sun! These are all natural satellites that formed in space. Artificial satellites, however, are machines made by humans. They are launched into space on a rocket. They can orbit Earth or travel around another celestial object.

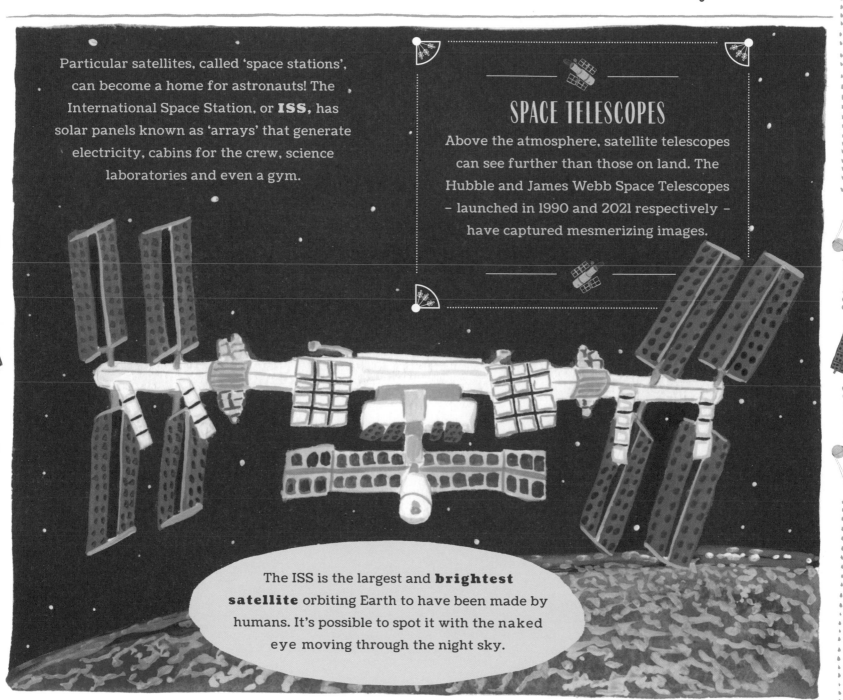

Particular satellites, called 'space stations', can become a home for astronauts! The International Space Station, or **ISS**, has solar panels known as 'arrays' that generate electricity, cabins for the crew, science laboratories and even a gym.

SPACE TELESCOPES

Above the atmosphere, satellite telescopes can see further than those on land. The Hubble and James Webb Space Telescopes – launched in 1990 and 2021 respectively – have captured mesmerizing images.

The ISS is the largest and **brightest satellite** orbiting Earth to have been made by humans. It's possible to spot it with the naked eye moving through the night sky.

CONNECTING EARTH FROM SPACE

These human-made space objects can also help to reveal your exact location on Earth. The Global Positioning System, or GPS, is a group of more than thirty satellites that communicate with a GPS receiver (for example, on a mobile phone) to help you navigate. Others allow you to watch TV, use the internet and make phone calls. Communications satellites receive signals from TVs and phones from Earth, and send them back down to another part of the planet.

WATCHING EARTH

Artificial satellites not only help us to learn more about the Solar System and the universe – they also allow us to explore our own home in it.

The first photo of Earth taken by a satellite came from the American Explorer 6, launched in 1959.

From their own paths around our home planet, our heroes can observe very large areas at once. This is a huge advantage compared to other instruments on land, which can only see so much at a time.

The scientific instruments on satellites collect information about Earth's land, water, ice, air and atmosphere. This allows scientists to study our planet throughout the years – for example, to learn about how its climate is changing.

From space, satellites can also help to predict the weather. With information obtained from satellites, farmers have a better idea of what crops to plant and when, and how to better manage water. Some satellites also keep an eye on volcanoes' eruptions, wildfires, hurricanes and other natural disasters.

MEET THE SPACE STATION →

Humans have always been explorers. Since the first successful satellite was launched, we have planned ever-more ambitious missions. In the year 2000, a major goal was finally achieved – the International Space Station became home to the first live-in crew, giving us a permanent base in outer space.

HOW TO SPOT SATELLITES

The working and living space on the ISS is as large as a six-bedroom house. The easiest satellite to spot in the night sky, it orbits Earth once every 90 minutes, travelling at a speed of 28,000 kilometers per hour.

So, how to know if what you are seeing is the ISS or something else, like a fast plane? First, remember that satellites don't have flashing lights like airplanes. The ISS can be more easily spotted close to sunrise or sunset. At its most luminous, the space station can glow as strongly as Venus, and many times brighter than the star Sirius.

What you can see is actually the light of the Sun reflected on its solar arrays. During the short summer nights in the northern hemisphere, sunlight illuminates the ISS longer. If you are patient, you can see it passing over your head several times.

Venus

ISS trajectory

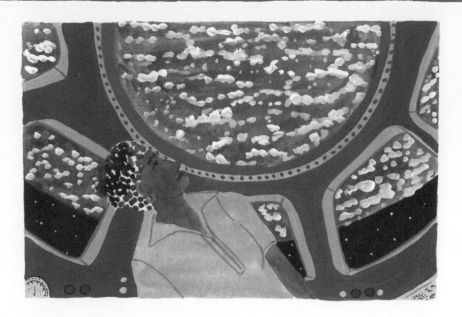

Building the International Space Station was a huge global effort. Thousands of engineers from many countries constructed the different parts on Earth. Then, these were sent into space on rockets. And astronauts put them together in space!

The ISS has been inhabited since 2000, orbiting more than 400 kilometres above Earth. On board, at least 6 humans at a time live in microgravity (very low gravity). The space station is mainly a laboratory in space – astronauts conduct research that benefits life on Earth. They also study how living in space affects the human body.

SATELLITES: A BRIEF HISTORY

The Soviet Union launched the first artificial satellite, **Sputnik 1**, in 1957, sparking the Space Race between the U.S. and Soviet Union.

A month later, the Soviet Union launched **Sputnik 2**. It carried a dog! Laika, a stray from the streets of Moscow, became the first living creature from Earth in space.

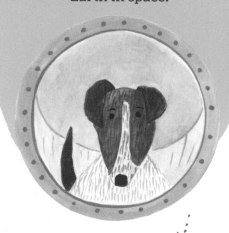

In 1990, the Hubble Space Telescope was put into orbit, giving us a breathtaking glimpse of deep space. In 2021, the **James Webb Space Telescope** was launched and is already sending spectacular images.

On 12th April 1961 **Yuri Gagarin** became the first human in space, completing one orbit around Earth in a capsule called *Vostok 1* before returning safely – and making history.

In 1960, NASA launched **TIROS-1**, the first-ever full-scale weather satellite.

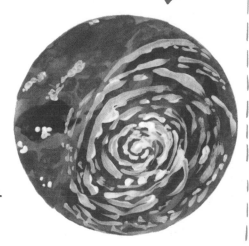

ACRUX

the HERO OF TRAVEL and TRADITION

Acrux is the brightest star in the Southern Cross.
This beloved cross made out of stars
is an important symbol in the
southern hemisphere.

Acrux glows in one end of the Southern Cross, an asterism also known as the Crux constellation. Our hero is one of the four bright stars that form the celestial cross. Even though Crux is the smallest (in area) of the 88 official constellations, it is one of the most familiar sights in the southern night skies.

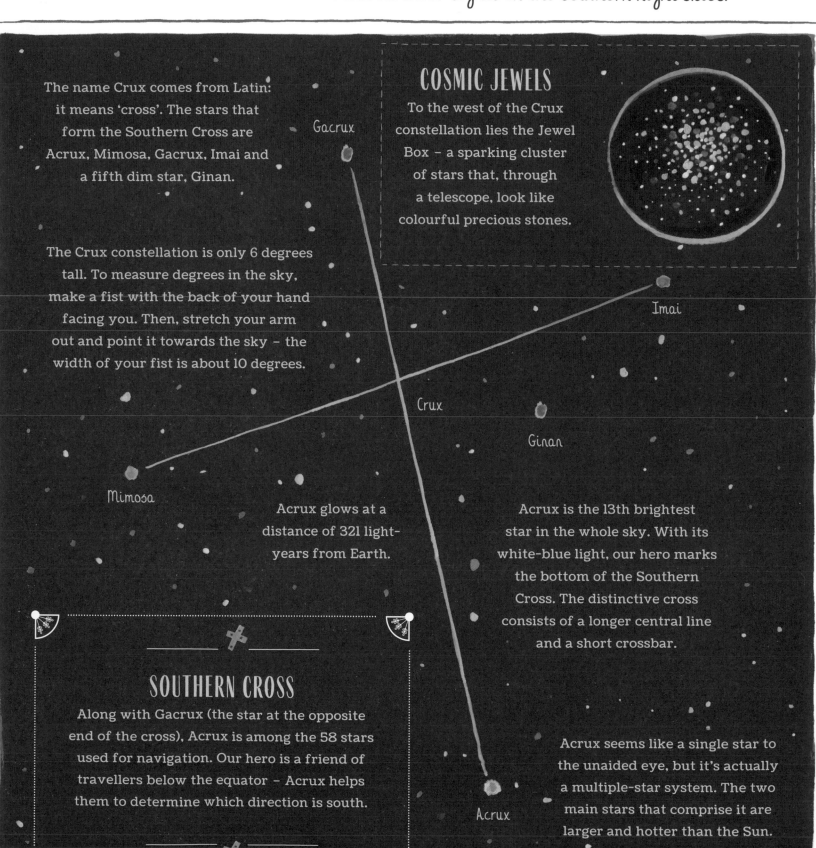

The name Crux comes from Latin: it means 'cross'. The stars that form the Southern Cross are Acrux, Mimosa, Gacrux, Imai and a fifth dim star, Ginan.

The Crux constellation is only 6 degrees tall. To measure degrees in the sky, make a fist with the back of your hand facing you. Then, stretch your arm out and point it towards the sky – the width of your fist is about 10 degrees.

COSMIC JEWELS

To the west of the Crux constellation lies the Jewel Box – a sparking cluster of stars that, through a telescope, look like colourful precious stones.

Gacrux

Imai

Crux

Ginan

Mimosa

Acrux glows at a distance of 321 light-years from Earth.

Acrux is the 13th brightest star in the whole sky. With its white-blue light, our hero marks the bottom of the Southern Cross. The distinctive cross consists of a longer central line and a short crossbar.

SOUTHERN CROSS

Along with Gacrux (the star at the opposite end of the cross), Acrux is among the 58 stars used for navigation. Our hero is a friend of travellers below the equator – Acrux helps them to determine which direction is south.

Acrux

Acrux seems like a single star to the unaided eye, but it's actually a multiple-star system. The two main stars that comprise it are larger and hotter than the Sun.

POINTING SOUTH

For hundreds of years, sailors cruising the southern waters have used the Southern Cross as a marker in the sky.

People in the northern hemisphere can count on a single star, Polaris, to find the north celestial pole.

The nearest visible star to the south celestial pole is Polaris Australis (Sigma Octantis). This star is too faint though, so it's not very useful to travellers trying to make their way on land, air or sea.

Instead, the southern half of the world relies on a group of stars, the Southern Cross, to find the south celestial pole (the point in the sky around which all southern stars appear to rotate around).

To locate the celestial south pole, simply draw an imaginary line connecting the 'top' of the cross (the star Gacrux) to the 'bottom' of it (the star Acrux). Then, extend that line about four times the distance between Gacrux and Acrux.

MEET THE CONSTELLATION

Nowadays, Crux is not visible from most of the northern hemisphere – but a few thousand years ago, that wasn't the case.

The ancient Greeks were able to see Crux clearly, although they considered it to be a part of a different constellation: Centaurus.

What happened later is due to 'precession' – the wobble of Earth's axis – which causes stars to slowly move across the sky. This movement led Crux to shift over a long period of time, making it visible in the southern skies.

HOW TO SPOT ACRUX

Acrux, along with the rest of the stars in the Southern Cross, is visible throughout the year in the southern skies. The celestial cross is easy to find – it is one of the most recognizable shapes for stargazers in this part of Earth.

The Crux constellation can be seen from some locations in the northern hemisphere, closer to the equator – the further south you are, the higher in the sky you'll find it. But, for most of the northern half of the planet, the Southern Cross doesn't rise above the horizon and remains invisible.

ACRUX: A BRIEF HISTORY

'Acrux' is the combination of '**A**' (Alpha) and '**Crux**' – the name was given by the American astronomer Elijah Hinsdale Burritt in the 1800s. He wrote accessible texts to help ordinary people learn about the sky. The name Acrux was officially approved in 2016.

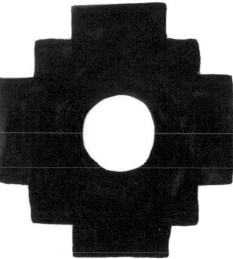

The Inca knew the Crux constellation as **Chakana**, which in Quechua means 'the bridge' or 'the stairs'. One of its many interpretations is that it connected the Andean people to the cosmos.

The Southern Cross has different meanings across New Zealand. The indigenous Māori people know it by several names. Some saw it as *Te Punga*, an **anchor** of a great sky canoe. Others as *Māhutonga*, an opening in the Milky Way through which winds escaped.

The stars of the Southern Cross are found in the **flags** of Australia, New Zealand, Brazil, Papua New Guinea, and others. In Brazil, it is known as *Cruzeiro do Sul* – it is even mentioned in the national anthem.

In Aboriginal Australian astronomy, the cross and the dark patch between its stars (the Coalsack Nebula) represent the head of the **Emu** in the Sky. In Aboriginal legend, these birds were spirits associated with different myths about creation.

THE MILKY WAY

the HERO OF IMMENSITY *and* ANCESTRY

Earth is our home in the Solar System, where the Sun is the only star.

But the Sun is just one among many, many millions of stars in our galaxy, which we call the Milky Way.

THE MILKY WAY
OUR GALAXY

The Milky Way galaxy is our home in the immense universe. A galaxy is an enormous collection of stars, planets, dust and gas – all held together in space by the force of gravity. All the stars and planets that you can spot are part of the Milky Way. Because we are inside the galaxy, we cannot see it as a whole – but we can glimpse portions of it.

THE LOCAL GROUP

Our galaxy is part of a cluster, or group, of over 30 galaxies called the Local Group. One of these galaxies is Andromeda, the largest spiral galaxy closest to the Milky Way. Our galactic neighbour is about two million light-years away.

Most of the stars in the Milky Way are thought to have planets orbiting them. Scientists have discovered thousands of planets outside our Solar System called 'exoplanets'.

Our galaxy is so colossal that it takes light at least **87,000 years** to travel across it.

In space, everything is moving! While Earth orbits the Sun, the Solar System orbits the centre of the Milky Way – a black hole called **Sagittarius A***.

The Milky Way has **four main spiral 'arms'** that extend from the centre.

We live in a smaller arm called the **Orion Arm**, halfway between the heart of the galaxy and the outer edges.

FUTURE COLLISION

Even though the universe is huge, galaxies do bump into each other sometimes. The Milky Way and Andromeda will eventually crash – but the collision won't happen for more than four billion years.

The Milky Way was born long before our planet formed. Our galaxy is roughly as old as the universe: over 13 billion years old.

Spiral

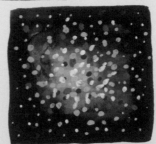

Irregular

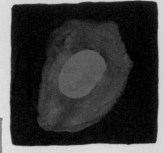

Elliptical

Galaxies are like islands of stars in the cosmos. They come in many sizes and different shapes. Spiral galaxies like the Milky Way look like bright pinwheels. Other galaxies are oval-shaped – these are called 'elliptical galaxies'. Others have irregular shapes.

In 1927, Dutch astronomer Jan Oort confirmed that the Milky Way rotates around its centre. Scientists think that at the heart of most galaxies there is a supermassive black hole.

A black hole is a dense region of space where the pull of gravity is extremely strong. The black hole at the heart of the Milky Way is four million times more massive than the Sun! In 2022, astronomers revealed the first image of it. It's not possible to see a black hole because it's completely dark, but using telescopes, astronomers can observe a dark region called the 'shadow', surrounded by slowly swirling matter and bended light.

MEET THE GALAXY

Until recently, astronomers thought our galaxy was alone... In the 1920s, American astronomer Edwin Hubble confirmed that's not the case: there are more galaxies in the vast universe that we can count! The iconic Hubble Space Telescope was launched in 1990 and it has helped study how galaxies form, evolve and interact with each other.

Piecing together the Milky Way hasn't been easy. Scientists are still learning about its structure and size. A space telescope called Gaia (launched in 2013) has been charting millions of stars in the Milky Way. Gaia is working on a three-dimensional map of our galaxy!

The powerful James Webb Space Telescope (launched in 2021) was designed to see through cosmic dust. It can take images of the first stars and galaxies, that developed shortly after the universe formed. Studying how other galaxies were born and have changed over time helps us to learn more about the past and future of our own galactic home.

THE MILKY WAY: A BRIEF HISTORY

Throughout time, different cultures have told stories that explain the mysterious whitish glow arcing across the night sky.

For the **ancient Greeks**, it was created by the goddess Hera, Zeus's wife, who sprayed milk across the heavens.

HOW TO SPOT THE MILKY WAY

The Milky Way appears as a glowing, dusty cloud stretching across the night sky.

What you see is part of the Orion Arm, the area of the galaxy that holds our Solar System. This long band of light is actually the light of millions of distant stars. They are so far away that their light blends together.

To see the Milky Way in all its glory, you need really dark skies. This often means being far away from light pollution caused by artificial lights from cities.

In the northern hemisphere, the best time of the year to spot the Milky Way is summer. You can get a better view of our galaxy from the southern skies, where the stream of light appears larger and brighter. (This is because you're looking towards the galactic centre, where there is more gas, dust and stars.)

The **Romans** also saw the band of light in the skies as divine liquid. They called it the *Via Lactea*, which means the 'road made of milk'.

The Finns and Estonians call the hazy band of light '**Pathway of the Birds**'. They observed that some birds used the stars to navigate the skies when migrating, or travelling, south.

In **China**, the Milky Way is known as the 'Silver River'.

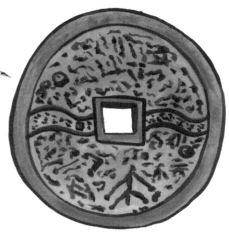

In **Māori** mythology, the Milky Way is *Te Māngōroa*, a shark placed in the sky by Māui, a demigod (half god, half human).

THE ATMOSPHERE

the HERO
PAGEANTRY
and
PROTECTION

When you look up at night, you're seeing space through a very special window: Earth's atmosphere. Without this multilayered blanket, life on our planet wouldn't exist.

THE ATMOSPHERE
AIR

Earth is wrapped by the atmosphere: layers of gases vital to living things. The atmosphere contains the air we breathe. It protects us from the Sun's harmful rays. It's our shield from asteroids. It makes the stars twinkle and gifts us with breathtaking auroras.

Earth's atmosphere is made up of gases such as oxygen, nitrogen, carbon dioxide, ozone and water vapour.

Our atmosphere has five main layers...

1. The **exosphere** is the outermost layer of our atmosphere. But where exactly does Earth end and space begin? It turns out there is no clear answer. Typically, it is said that space begins at about 100 kilometres above the surface.

2. Satellites with a low Earth orbit – including the International Space Station – are in the **thermosphere**. This is also where the Northern and Southern Lights occur.

3. Most meteors burn up in the **mesosphere** (making meteor showers a brilliant show). If our planet didn't have an atmosphere, it would be heavily pockmarked like the surface of the Moon!

4. The **stratosphere** is where the famous (and beloved) ozone layer is. It shields Earth against ultraviolet radiation from the Sun. This type of solar energy can be harmful to life on Earth.

5. The **troposphere** extends up to 18 kilometres from Earth's surface. That might not seem too high – but this layer contains all the air we need to live. This is also where most of our weather takes place.

TWINKLE, TWINKLE

Stars look like they're **twinkling** – but they are not. When starlight passes through the moving air in the atmosphere it gets refracted, or bended, in many directions. This causes the star to look like it's flickering.

SOLAR WIND

The Northern and Southern Lights may seem magical but scientists can explain what makes them appear.

It all starts with the Sun! Our closest star creates solar wind, which then carries tiny particles called protons and electrons.

Along with the atmosphere, the Earth is surrounded by a magnetic field that protects us from the streams of high-energy particles coming from the Sun. Usually, when the solar wind runs into Earth, the magnetic field forces the particles to go around our planet.

But when the solar wind is very strong, these particles can get past the magnetic field. Then, the magnetic field leads the particles to Earth's poles. And at some point, the particles collide with the atmosphere, releasing their energy in the form of light. That's when the Northern and Southern Lights happen!

When the solar wind particles smash into the oxygen in our atmosphere, we see green and red light, while nitrogen makes blue and purple.

MEET THE ATMOSPHERE

Using satellites from Earth and in space, scientists study and monitor our atmosphere. They keep track of how it's changing – and try to predict how it will be in the future.

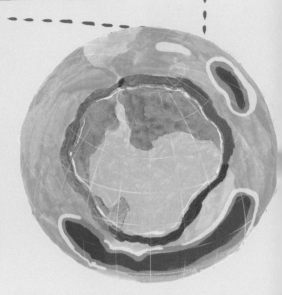

HOW TO SPOT THE AURORAS

The Northern and Southern Lights take place near the magnetic poles. This means the colourful display is better seen in places closer to these locations – so catching the show might involve a trip! In the north, these destinations include Alaska, Greenland, Siberia, Norway and Sweden. The Southern Lights are better seen from Antarctica. They can also illuminate the skies in places like New Zealand, Australia, and the south of Chile and Argentina.

The best time of the year to enjoy the auroras is in winter, around midnight. You need dark and clear skies to see them in all their glory. You should find a spot away from city lights. Also keep in mind the phases of the Moon – too much moonlight might spoil the unforgettable view.

A few decades ago, scientists discovered that the ozone layer was being depleted. They realized that the 'hole' in the layer was being made by harmful chemicals used by humans. Countries around the world came together and agreed to gradually eliminate these chemicals. The agreement is called the Montreal Protocol. Not long ago, scientists confirmed that the actions taken are working – the ozone layer is recovering.

Some gases in the atmosphere, like carbon dioxide, help our Earth to stay warm.

They do so by trapping some of the heat from the Sun – a process known as the 'greenhouse effect'. But human activity (like fossil-fuel burning) increases the greenhouse effect, leading to global warming. A warmer planet harms the environment and affects us all.

ATMOSPHERE: A BRIEF HISTORY

The scientific term for the Northern Lights is **aurora borealis**. The name was given by the famous astronomer Galileo more than 400 years ago. The term combines the name of the Roman goddess of the dawn (Aurora) and the word 'borealis', which means 'northern'. The Southern Lights are called **aurora australis**.

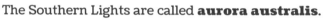

The **Menominee Tribe** of Wisconsin in the USA saw the Northern Lights as the torches of manabai'wok – giants who were great hunters and fishermen. The giants' light in the sky showed them where to go fishing.

In Finland, the Northern Lights are known as *revontulet*, which means **'fox fires'**. In Finnish folklore, the firefox is a mythical creature. When it runs, its tail brushes against the trees and creates sparks that set the sky on fire.

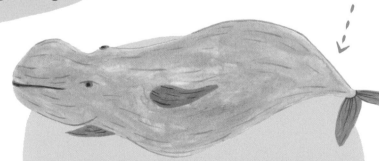

To some **Inuit** groups in Alaska, the brilliant lights were the spirits of the animals they had hunted: salmon, beluga whales, seals and deers.

GLOSSARY

ASTERISM - a small pattern of stars within a constellation

ASTEROID – a chunk of rock that orbits the Sun

ATMOSPHERE - the layer of gases that surround a planet

BLACK HOLE - a region of space where the pull of gravity is so strong that even light cannot escape

CELESTIAL POLE - a region above Earth's poles where stars appear to revolve

COMET - a huge, frozen ball of gas, rock, and dust in space

CONSTELLATION - a group of stars that form a shape in the sky

CRATER - a large hollow in the surface of a celestial object, often caused by the impact of a meteorite

ELECTRON - a negatively charged subatomic particle

ELLIPTICAL - oval-shaped

EQUATOR - an imaginary line around the centre of the Earth

GALAXY - a huge collection of stars, planets and matter, held together by gravity

GRAVITY - a force that attracts matter together

GREENHOUSE EFFECT - when gases in Earth's atmosphere trap the Sun's rays, heating our planet

LIGHT-YEAR - the distance that light travels in a year

MAGNETIC FIELD - a region of space where magnetic forces can be felt

MASS - the amount of matter within an object that determines grativational pull

METEOR - a space rock passing through Earth's atmosphere, appearing as a streak of light

METEORITE - a space rock that lands on Earth's surface

METEOROID - a small body travelling through space

MOON - a natural satellite that orbits a planet

NEBULA - a huge cloud of dust and gas in space

ORBIT - a circular or oval-shaped path that one object in space takes around another

OZONE LAYER - a layer of gas that protects Earth from the Sun's ultraviolet rays

PLANET - a spherical object that orbits the Sun

PROTON - a postively charged subatomic particle

PROTOSTAR - a young star which cannot yet fuse hydrogen atoms into helium

RADIOACTIVE - emitting radiation from a nuclear reaction

SATELLITE - a celestial or human-made object that orbits a larger object

SOLAR SYSTEM - the Sun and all the objects that orbit it.

SOLAR WIND - a stream of particles from the sun

STAR - a luminous, burning ball of gas held together by its own gravity

ULTRAVIOLET - electromagnetic radiation with a short wavelength, invisible to the human eye

WHITE DWARF — a small, dense star that is running out of fuel and glows less brightly

FURTHER READING

Links to online resources to learn more:

Constellation Guide – constellation-guide.com

Earth Sky – earthsky.org

European Southern Observatory – eso.org/public

European Space Agency – esa.int/kids/en/home

Exploratorium – exploratorium.edu

Griffith Observatory – griffithobservatory.org

Little Astronomy – littleastronomy.com

Lunar and Planetary Institute – lpi.usra.edu

NASA's Space Place – spaceplace.nasa.gov

National Geographic Society – kids.nationalgeographic.com

Natural History Museum – nhm.ac.uk

Royal Museums Greenwich – rmg.co.uk

Space.com – space.com

To Olivia, my brightest star – N.G.
For my two shining stars, Jaiah and Francis – S.B.M.

MAGIC CAT PUBLISHING

Glow © 2023 Lucky Cat Publishing Ltd
Text © 2023 Noelia González
Illustrations © 2023 Sara Boccaccini Meadows
First Published in 2023 by Magic Cat Publishing, an imprint of Lucky Cat Publishing Ltd
Unit 2, Empress Works, 24 Grove Passage, London E2 9FQ

The right of Noelia González to be identified as the author of this work and
Sara Boccaccini Meadows to be identified as the illustrator of this work has been asserted by
them in accordance with the Copyright, Designs and Patents Act, 1988 (UK).

No part of this publication may be reproduced, stored in a retrieval system, or transmitted,
in any form, or by any means, electrical, mechanical, photocopying, recording or otherwise
without the prior written permission of the publisher or a licence permitting restricted copying.

A catalogue record for this book is available from the British Library.

ISBN 978-1-913520-78-6

The illustrations were created in watercolour and gouache paints.
Set in A Thousand Years, Coustard, Farmhand, Haute and Moonflower

Published by Rachel Williams and Jenny Broom
Designed by Nicola Price

Manufactured in China, TLF0123

9 8 7 6 5 4 3 2 1

FSC MIX Paper from responsible sources FSC® C104723

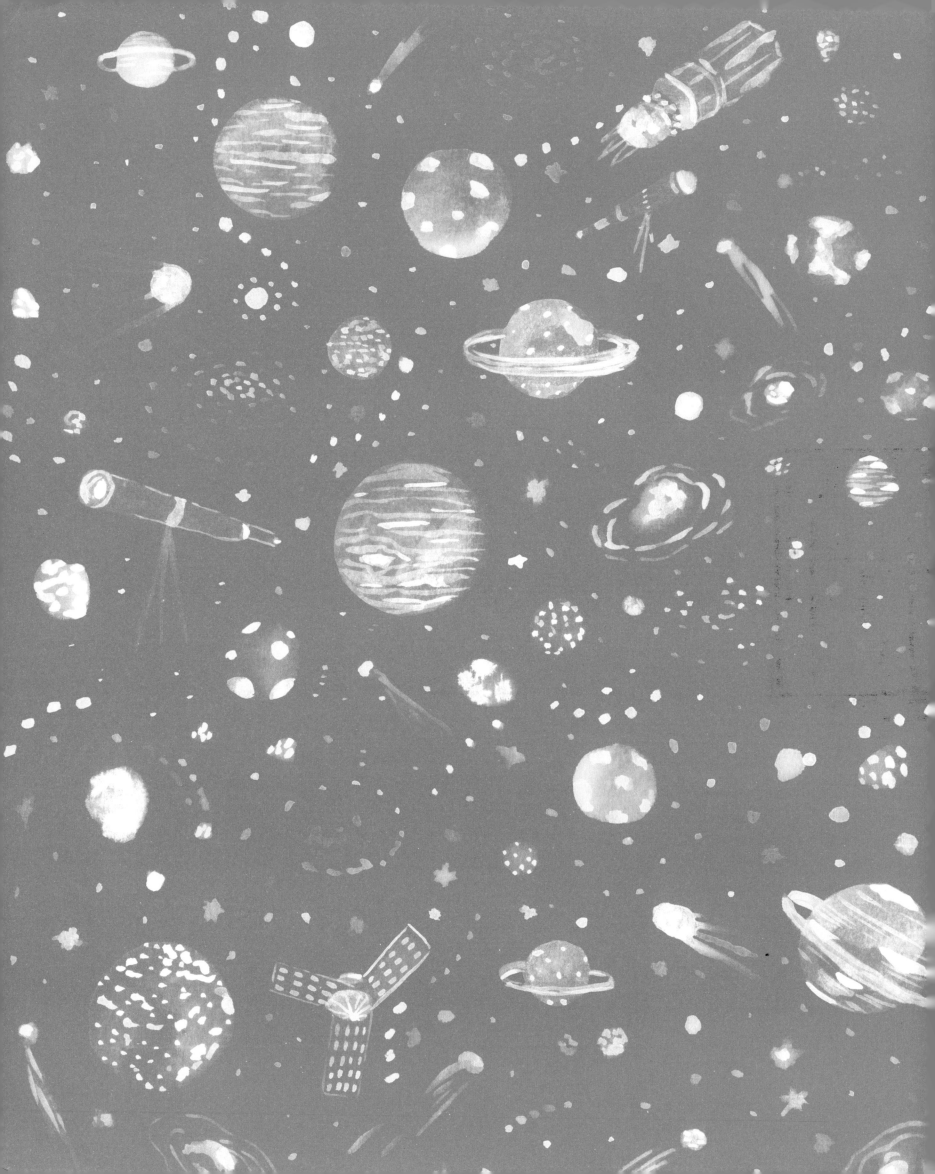